HABITAT IN THE PAST:
HISTORICAL PERSPECTIVES OF
RIPARIAN ZONES ON THE WHITE RIVER

Frederic J. Athearn

Colorado State Office
Denver, Colorado
1988

TABLE OF CONTENTS

FOREWORD

This document represents the results of a unique concept called Project EXCEL. Several years ago, it was decided to establish a program that would allow Bureau of Land Management employees in Colorado to expand their jobs and visibility by giving them the time and resources needed to develop special projects. Project EXCEL is designed to provide the necessary time for the development of creative concepts in land management. EXCEL projects are chosen by a management committee that reviews all applications. When a project is selected for development, the employee is given a block of time and adequate funding to work on his/her idea. The final product is presented to the committee for approval. Many, if not all, Project EXCEL products are implemented for daily use.

There have been numerous Projects EXCEL over the last several years, ranging from archaeological protection to wildlife management. This represents the first Project EXCEL to be published. I hope that the readers of this work will find it of use. Most importantly, it can be of value in understanding land management. By printing this work, it can be distributed throughout the Bureau. It can also be provided to the public in order to increase understanding as to how our past relates to the present.

I am pleased to make available Dr. Frederic J. Athearn's Project EXCEL to both Bureau employees and to the general public. I trust that you will find it both enjoyable and useful.

State Director, Colorado

ACKNOWLEDGEMENTS

A number of people assisted in the preparation of this report and in providing direction for this project. The Project EXCEL committee, made up of Ken Witt, Carl Buchanan, Frank Young, and Bill Pulford are all to be thanked for their patience and understanding over the two years it took to research and write this study. Assistance from the U.S. Geological Survey Photo Library, the Colorado State Historical Society, and the Rangley, Colorado Historical Society is gratefully acknowledged. Without their kind help this project would not have been possible.

Several individuals provided special assistance that deserves mention. First, Andy Senti of the Colorado State Office helped greatly in the search for survey records. He also did excellent editorial work on the draft manuscript. Mike Selle, White River Resource Area archaeologist, went out of his way to locate the areas that were rephotographed. Mike spent many hours finding out where the photos were taken and then assisted in our field work. His help is very greatly appreciated. Additionally, Jerry Harman and Dale Brubaker of the Branch of Biological Resources, Colorado State Office, provided much assistance by developing the idea for this project, based on Quentin Skinner's article and in providing comments on the drafts of this work. Their continued support is also greatly appreciated, as is that of Gary McVicker, Deputy State Director, Division of Lands and Renewable Resources, Colorado State Office, who provided literature cited in this report. Dudley Gardner of Western Wyoming College kindly provided photographs. And last, but not least, a special thanks to Anna Aytes who typed the manuscript, reorganized it and made some excellent editorial suggestions.

Cover Photo: The Strawberry Creek Basin, Rio Blanco County, Colorado, drains into the White River. Photo Courtesy: U.S. Geological Survey.

INTRODUCTION

Traditionally, it has been assumed that riparian habitat, that is the vegetation along streambanks, was in better condition a hundred years ago than it is today. However, various studies conducted recently by agencies such as the Bureau of Land Management, by private landowners, and by academic institutions have caused this assumption to be questioned. Historically, riparian areas were the first to be settled by the oncoming mass of pioneers headed westward. This makes sense because European settlers followed natural (and usually easy) courses west. Since most immigrants were seeking land that was agricultural in nature, they desired places that could be irrigated. This meant that most early settlement happened along watercourses.

On the high plains, there were few areas that had natural watercourses. They were quickly claimed as farmsteads and after 1863, homesteads. Needless to say, land speculators and others bought up land along rivers from the government at the standard rate of $1.25 per acre and then resold it to would-be farmers. Hence, the bottomlands were quickly taken up and used for settlement, agriculture, and irrigation. It is no coincidence that towns were platted along streams, nor is it surprising that most colonies (like the Greeley Union Colony) were established along waterways. Irrigation was vital in a dry climate such as was found west of the 100th meridian which bisects the Great Plains in Kansas on a north-south line. It was also true that the easiest routes for settlers were along the waterways. A natural wagon/horse passage was created for immigrants by many river valleys. It was much easier to follow the streams than it was to go directly overland. This was particularly true when immigrants reached the Rockies. The canyons and rivers were the only natural trails through the mountains. This is the primary reason that the Oregon Trail ,for example, went through Wyoming. The passage over the Continental Divide at this point was much easier than through the Colorado Rockies.

Obviously, there are exceptions to this observation. For example, hard rock mining was no respecter of watercourses when it came to extracting gold or silver, but ranching and farming were totally dependent upon available water and timber resources. That water (and the subsequent riparian area) was important was seen in California by 1849 and the discovery of gold there. Because the mineral was placer in nature, water was vital to its recovery. The resultant fights over water caused a strict code of water rights to be established in the west. Aridity, one of the worst problems for settlers, was resolved by the development of water laws that allocated water and prioritized its use. Unlike the east, where there was plenty of water, the west was much harder to develop. Back east, water rights were not a major problem, out west they were.

Historically, waterways were used by explorers, fur traders, soldiers, settlers, and just about everyone else who had to traverse the western landscape. Because of this fact, there were a number of journals and descriptive texts generated by those who visited the west. The opportunity for historians to gain an understanding of what the environment looked like 150 years ago is contained in these documents. Unlike today where we have environmental statements that give us a very detailed "slice" of the land and its resources for a specific parcel, we can only speculate as to exactly what the west might have looked like in the past. In order to compare the past with today, a genre called "rephotography" has developed during the last twenty years. Some examples of this are the 1984 study by Garry Rogers, Harold Malde and Raymond Turner in which a bibliography of repeat photography has been created. In 1979 the Bureau of Land Management, Montana State Office, published a comparative photography volume of the Missouri Breaks in Montana that showed vegetative changes using old and new photos. Another study called *Second View* by Mark Klett details a rephotographic survey project conducted in 1984.[1]

The use of photography to compare environmental conditions is an excellent method in which to accurately evaluate riparian habitat past and present. While rephotography has occurred for landscapes, comparing soil erosion and riparian vegetation may be a new use of research and photography. By combining records such as journals with photographs that are available for a given geographic area, one can reconstruct what the environment may have been like. There are inherent limitations in this methodology. First, who knows what the area really looked like? There is a great deal of subjective judgement on the part of the observer/writer. Depending on the purpose of the author, land descriptions can vary from a "moonscape" to the Garden of Eden. One would think that the government explorers would be unbiased in their descriptions of the land. However, this is not always true. Depending on land disposal policies of the time, the government was often the most vocal booster of western lands. Witness some of the reports generated by John W. Powell and later U.S. Geological surveys that are boosterish and glowingly describe areas that are less than ideal for agriculture. Of course, this would help settle the region with homesteaders if the place sounded good. Contrary to popular belief, the government encouraged the disposal of the public domain as quickly as possible. This was the principal mission of the General Land Office (GLO) from its establishment into the 20th century.

A second obvious problem in reconstruction of the environment is that photographs are not available very far back. The use of photography in the west became prominent with the Ferdinand V. Hayden surveys of the 1870s and photos by William Henry Jackson. Jackson photographed scenes that had theretofore been drawn by artists.[2] While artists' paintings were often spectacular, they were not always accurate. The official artists probably tried to be as realistic as possible, but commercial painters such as Albert Bierstadt portrayed the western landscape in truly titanic proportions. Bierstadt canvasses invariably show riparian areas as lush and teeming with wildlife. Somehow, this seems to be overly exaggerated when compared to the journals of the time.

A third problem lies in the fact that there are thousands of miles of riparian habitat in the west. To discuss this much land would be virtually impossible. Therefore, the scope of any comparative study must be narrowed and refined. For the purpose of this project, the White River drainage, running from west of Meeker, Colorado to the Utah state line was selected because it met several criteria established to limit the parameters of the study. The criteria, briefly, are: 1) the drainage must have BLM lands near its banks or in the secondary drainages, 2) the river must be in reasonably "natural" condition; that is, there should be a minimum amount of disturbance such as dams, etc., 3) a body of literature should exist pertaining

to the river, 4) historic photographs should be available to provide comparisons between previous conditions and current status, and 5) the area should have sufficient documentation about vegetation and soils to aid in comparisons.

The land along the White River, from just west of Meeker to the state line, is mostly BLM. While the bottomland is private, the side drainages and most of the steeper canyon area is BLM down to the river. The White River has not been substantially altered over the years. There is one dam along the White at Taylor Draw. The dike at Rio Blanco reservoir diverts the White, but does not dam it. There are some irrigation headgates along the streambank, but few other alterations have occurred. There is a body of literature pertaining to the White River region that is readily available. This includes journals, exploration records, and other documents, including both secondary and primary records ranging from articles to books. The White, while not as famous as some other streams, nevertheless has been well known to travelers in the region.

Documentation dates from 1776 with the Dominguez-Escalante Expedition and continues to the present. This makes the White one of the "best known" streams in the west by virtue of longevity. During the late 19th century and well into the present, U.S. Geological Survey geologists/photographers worked in the region of the White. Minerals from oil shale to natural gas have been well studied in this area. The field geologists were inveterate photographers, leaving a wealth of images of the region they visited. The Geologic Survey maintains the photos in its Denver Library where they can be viewed and/or copied. Finally, there has been much study and recordation of vegetation and soil conditions in this area. As part of the Bureau of Land Management's ongoing range program (management for wildlife and domestic grazing), vegetation studies are available. Additionally, the potential development of oil shale spawned a number of detailed Environmental Statements that contain valuable vegetation and soils data. Oil and gas development, along with several major coal mines, also generated considerable environmental/geographic information that is useful for a project such as this.

METHODOLOGY

In order to derive enough data for descriptions of the environment, it was necessary to first define the data base. This was done by means of assessing general literature that is commonly available, including subject studies, regional histories, environmental impact statements, land use plans, and by determining the availability of these works.[3] Of value in a project such as this are journals and diaries written by those who were in the region at various times.

Information on the White River country is fairly easy to find because it has been known to Europeans since 1776. The Dominguez-Escalante Expedition of that year left us with detailed notes about this region. Equally, the fur trappers wrote journals that give some general descriptions of the White, which was trapped during the 1830s. Perhaps of more value are the official government surveys. John Charles Fremont's notes are not particularly useful because they are so sketchy. However, Ferdinand V. Hayden's surveys of the 1870s provide much detailed descriptive material about this region. John Wesley Powell's notes are not very useful because he really was not interested in the White River, but rather the Green.

Other descriptions can be found in the notes and diaries of the various Indian agents that lived at White River Agency. Danforth and Meeker, for example, left journals that described life at the agency. Some environmental data is therefore preserved, although it is sketchy and not overly useful. Of most value are the cadastral survey notes that were prepared by the surveyors who actually were "on the ground" and recorded what they saw. In the case of the White River country, this survey work dates to 1883. While the early surveys, which were made under contract, may have been fraudulent, the data is consistent with later survey work. The resurveys of the early 1900s are also quite specific and are known to be accurate as indicated in their acceptance by the General Land Office.

The U.S. Geological Survey did much mineral and geological survey work in this region at the turn of the 20th century. The reports that were generated contain descriptive materials, although most of the information is geologic in nature. These reports were published in the USGS's series of Bulletins over the years. Of perhaps more value than the reports are the photographs that were also taken at this time. These photos give a view of the region's topography and vegetation. The photos, located in the USGS Photo Library, are one of the most valuable assets in a project such as this.

Other sources include the Colorado Historical Society which has a good collection of primary and secondary materials including photographs, articles, and books. The older articles in the *Colorado Magazine* are useful in obtaining descriptions of life and times in the area through the eyes of "old timers."

There are also local sources such as newspapers, county records, and historical societies that may have materials. Generally, however, they do not have environmental data, but rather are interested in historical events of the region. Sometimes, as in the case of Rio Blanco County, these local sources have been compiled into volumes of memoirs and oral remembrances. In the case of the White River, the Bury's *This Is What I Remember*, and Dudley Gardner's *Oral Historical Accounts of Northwestern Colorado* provide useful oral histories containing environmental descriptions as told by pioneers.

Other useful materials include maps, both old and new, survey plats, drawings and sketches, and other graphic materials that can provide insight into what the environment looked like at a given point in time. Such data can be helpful for visual interpretation of a region or for a particular geographic feature.

Using 18 U.S. Geological Survey photographs, a field rephotographic survey was conducted in June, 1988. Sixteen of the original photos were relocated and photographed. Twelve photos were finally selected for this study. Given the problem of knowing exactly where the original photo was taken, what the focal length of the photographer's lens was, and the time of day the photo was exposed, the recreated photographs were made as closely as possible to the original photos in terms of perspective and angle of view. In some cases no major changes are noted, while in other situations, there have been dramatic changes in vegetation. The photo section (Appendix 1) illustrates these changes, or lack of change. One final complication that occured in rephotogaphing these areas was the lack of legal access. In several photos, because the vantage point of the original was on private land, access to recreate the photo was not practical. In this situation, the recreated photo(s) are as close to the original as possible. All of the "recreated" photos were exposed with a Nikon FM camera using 24mm, 35mm, and 75-150mm Nikor lenses. The film used was 35mm Kodak Plus-X rated at ASA/ISO 125. A medium yellow filter was used on all exposures. The film was processed in Kodak D-76 using a 1:1 dilution ratio. The final prints were made on Ilford Multigrade II paper using number 2 and number 3 MG filters.

SOME IDEAS FOR RESEARCHING THIS TOPIC

1. When choosing a stream or river to research, make sure that there is enough written material to provide adequate data for the project.

2. Use local source materials whenever possible. Local historical societies, county records, and local residents can often provide more useful data than can a State Historical Society or university libraries.

3. Secondary source materials (i.e. books, articles, etc.) are as valuable as primary materials (i.e. survey records, etc.) because they provide historic descriptions of an area based on eyewitness accounts. The fur trapping journals, for example, are not readily available in the original, but a published version will give the same data and are easily available through local libraries or interlibrary loan.

4. The use of comparative photos is highly desireable. When chosing photos to rephotograph, find images that can be easily relocated on the ground. The U.S. Geological Survey's photos are quite useful in this regard because they have geographic descriptions. Local historical society photos, while useful, may not be easy to relocate.

5. The assistance of field personnel is very helpful. Resource area office help is valuable because the people in the area know the local situation, can help provide leads to local sources, and can help in the relocation of photo points. This source of help is the most important part of a project of this nature.

HISTORIC DESCRIPTIONS OF THE WHITE RIVER

The first documented descriptions of the White River country occurred in 1776 when an expedition led by the Fransicisan friars, Atenencio Dominguez and Silvestre Velez de Escalante noted crossing what they called the "Rio San Clemente" on September 9, 1776. The Dominguez-Escalante expedition of that year came from Santa Fe, New Mexico with the purpose of blazing a trail to the missions of California.[4] The group crossed western Colorado searching for an "easy" passage to the coast. Guided by Ute Indians, the little party managed to find its way north across the Book Cliffs, over Douglas Pass, down Douglas Creek (they described the drainage as "Canon Pintado" [Painted Canyon] because of its numerous petroglyphs), and on to the White River. On September 9th they camped on the northern edge of this stream (about where Rangely, Colorado is located).[5] Their journal noted that: ". . . there is a middle-sized meadow of good pasturage. This river is middling and flows west through here, and the terrain adjacent to it offers no prospects for settlement."[6] Clearly, the good friars were not overly impressed by the White and its prospects. The description of "good pasturage" is consistent with well-developed riparian areas along a watercourse, although it is interesting to note that they considered the White "middling." This drainage is one of the larger rivers on the western slope of Colorado and drains a very large area. Perhaps the explorers were disappointed after having crossed the Colorado [Grand] River a few days previously. The next day, the expedition marched down the White on their way into Utah. They described the land west of their campsite as: ". . . rockless hills and brief plains with neither pasturage nor trees, and of very loose soil." This describes the Raven Park area just west of Rangely. Their diary notes that they stopped at "El Barranco" [Stinking Water Wash] which they said had ". . . neither water nor pasturage in it." The friars also noted that this region had many buffalo that "winter hereabouts."[7] This information was related by the Utes who accompanied the explorers.

From the time of the Dominguez-Escalante expedition to the early 1820s, there are no particular records relating to the White River country. Because the land was inhabited by native Americans, and due to disputes over ownership of this area between Spain, Great Britain, and the United States, not many visitors crossed the region. After American independence occurred, there was great interest in the west.[8] By the early 19th century a fur trade had developed with numerous international traders working virtually every major stream west of the Mississippi. Their quarry was the beaver pelt which was used for hats in Europe.

The first records of fur trappers in the White River country appear in 1824 when Etienne Provost began working the White westward to the Green River in Utah. Provost is credited with "discovering" the Great Salt Lake in the early 1820s. He left no descriptions of this land, but in 1825 he met Jedediah Smith at the confluence of the White and Green Rivers.[9] Luckily, Smith was a literate trapper who left diaries that described the White River region from 1824-1826, the time he worked the area. Smith's descriptions, while rather general, nevertheless give a good idea what the place looked like at that time. Smith describes the "White River region" as ". . . high, rugged, barren mountains, the summits of which are either timbered with pine, quaking-asp [aspen], or cedar, or in fact, almost entirely destitute of vegetation."[10] This description is not far from what the White River valley looks like today. The "mountains" are more like hills; however, the lack of vegetation on the surrounding hills is quite accurate in the country from just east of Rangely, Colorado, to the Utah border.

Smith also described the region as: "Other parts are hilly and undulating; and the valleys and table lands (except on the borders of water courses which are more or less timbered with cotton-wood [sic] and willows) are destitute of wood . . . ."[11] Smith's descriptions of this region are consistent with other fur trader's observations. For instance, in 1822 William H. Ashley formed a new company to exploit the burgeoning fur trade. He proposed to trap the Green, the Bear and the White River areas. To get the new company going, he recruited men using the St. Louis, Missouri newspapers. His advertisements drew some of the greatest names in the fur business, including Thomas "Broken Hand" Fitzpatrick, Jim Bridger, William Sublette, Jedediah Smith and many others.

The new company made two expeditions west. The first, in 1822, was highly successful, followed by a second trip in 1825 that was equally profitable. Smith published his observations in the *St. Louis Enquirer* where he described the White River region as having ". . . sage, which grows from one to five feet high and is found in great abundance. . . . ."[12] He also noted that the soil was "sterile" and that there is little arable land despite rivers flowing . . . ."[13] He met with Etienne Provost in June 1825 on the White River, an area he said was "verry [sic] mountainous and barren."[14] Ashley's description of the Green River region south of the confluence with the White was equally unflattering. He condemned the place as ". . . a barren heap of rocky mountains."[15]

The fur trade died out in the late 1830s because of changing fashions in Europe (beaver hats were out of favor) and because of the depletion of the natural resources along the rivers. Beavers had nearly been wiped out by trapping. There were no major settlements in the region, although fur traders had established two "forts" that were used for trading. Antoine Robidoux's Fort Uintah was located in the White Rocks area of Utah. Robidoux and his men trapped and traded along the White River from Rangely to the Flat Tops. There are no specific records of this activity, thus there are no descriptions of the land. In Brown's Park, Prewett Sinclair, William Craig, and Phillip Thompson built Fort Davy Crockett along Vermillion Creek. This outpost of civilization was visited in 1839 by the German traveller F. A. Wislizenus who was less than complimentary about the fort and its surroundings. The place was abandoned by 1844 when John Charles Fremont passed through the region.[16] The significance of Fort Davy Crockett is that is represented the first permanent settlement in northwestern Colorado and it is well documented. Environmental and landscape descriptions are available from visitors to the fort, but this data is of limited use in the region of the White.

The 1840s saw a revival of exploration sponsored by the federal government because of changing conditions in the west. When Louisiana was acquired from France in 1803, President Thomas Jefferson had sent Zebulon M. Pike, and the Lewis and Clark expedition west to explore the newly acquired territory. In 1819 Stephen H. Long explored the front range of the Rockies in search of a trail to Santa Fe, New Mexico, and a passage

west. There was an expansionary mood in the country. Texas had been annexed, and Oregon was being settled at a very rapid pace. California was on the minds of Americans as being the last link in an "ocean to ocean" nation. It was natural that army explorers should go forth and seek paths west.

John Charles Fremont comes to mind as one of the premier explorers of the 1840s. Fremont was well connected politically, being married to Jessie Benton, Senator Thomas Hart Benton's daughter. It was not hard for Fremont to get commissions to explore the west. In 1843 he travelled from California eastward across Nevada and Utah to Colorado. He followed the White River into Colorado and turned north to Brown's Park from whence he crossed the plains of Wyoming. Fremont's next expedition came in 1845. He went west to California in that year by means of the White River. He crossed the Rockies near the headwaters of the Arkansas River and then followed the White River from its source to the Utah border. Fremont's journal and memoirs noted the White River country in minimal detail.[17]

Fremont's efforts were the last government explorations in the White River country until the 1870s. This did not mean, however, that others did not visit this region. In 1861, in response to the recent gold boom in the Clear Creek country, E. L. Berthoud surveyed a route from Golden City, Colorado to the Provo, Utah area. The purpose of the trip was to determine a practical route across the Rockies for either a road or railroad.[18]

Berthoud's survey (as opposed to an "expedition") was commercially sponsored and responded to various railway surveys that had occurred during the 1850s. A debate raged over where the proposed "transcontinental railroad" should go. Every state or territory, of course, wanted it to be built through its land. However, the Civil War intervened and stopped further serious debate about the line that could open the west. Colorado, fresh with enthusiasm from the Gold Rush that had just occurred, was convinced that it should have a transcontinental line, hence, the Berthoud survey.[19]

Berthoud proposed to travel up Clear Creek, over the Rockies west of Empire, Colorado, across Middle Park, over the Flat Tops and down the White River into Utah. This route, he felt, was not only much shorter than other known or proposed trails, but it was also "easy" to travel. Going over Berthoud Pass was the hardest part. If a railway was built, it would have to surmount the pass. The venture was described by the *Rocky Mountain News* in 1861. Berthoud's writings about the White River country are glowing. And why not? He was promoting a commercial route for a railroad that would bring settlement wherever it went. Settlers needed good land, so the White was going to be used for agriculture when the railroad was built.[20]

Berthoud detailed the route: ". . . the country towards the White and Grand Rivers becomes better watered, the land more fertile, and less predisposed to drought than the region north and towards the [Jim] Bridger and South Pass [Wyoming] routes;. . . ."[21] Berthoud was careful to note that: "the Valley of the White River presents large surfaces excellently adapted to agriculture and pastoral husbandry; and for salubrity, beauty of scenery and excellence of climate, will outstrip our region at the east side of the Rocky Mountains."[22] This picture of the White sounds too good to be true. It is hardly the White that the fur trappers and the Dominguez-Escalante expedition described. Boosterism had arrived on the White River. Contrary to the good friars' journal, Berthoud claims that there were large areas of pasture and flat lands for farming. To some extent this is true since the bottomlands offer irrigated areas that could be used for limited farming. However, the growing season is not long enough for vegetable farming, for instance. Berthoud's remarks about pastoral husbandry (i.e. ranching) are more on target. When settlement did occur, it was primarily for irrigated hay farming along the river.

Berthoud also noted that there were considerable mineral resources in the northwest section of Colorado. He stated that ". . . in the valleys of the Bear [Yampa] and White Rivers there is a vast coal field. . . ."[23] Others who had visited this area had made similar observations that were to be enlarged upon later. Since this survey was primarily to establish a route to Utah, Berthoud also concentrated on the virtues of the White River valley for immigrants and other travelers. Berthoud stated that his route was: "for an overland emigrant route, abundance of grassy prairies and meadows without the inconveniences of alkali or salitrose plains of the South Pass Route and the North Platte River".[24] These descriptions of the White River, as

an immigrant route, refer to the problems that travelers across Wyoming and Nebraska dealt with, primarily lack of good water and considerable areas of alkali. The White, it is true, was a constant flowing stream that was sweet water. However, crossing the Rockies was far more challenging than was Wyoming, a fact that Berthoud carefully overlooked. Grass was abundant along the White because this passage had never been used as an overland trail, thus the vegetation had not been depleted as occurred along the major migrations routes across Nebraska and Wyoming.[25]

Berthoud, ever the promoter, described the White River route again in 1866 as: "It (the route) pursues a river border continuously, through a country depress[ed] among mountains, covered and protected within them, fertile in soil and genial in temperature through the year."[26] Despite Berthoud's efforts at "selling" the White River route, there was no major road across the mountains and along this drainage. It was not until the removal of the Ute Indians in 1881 that the White River country was fully opened to European settlement. The White River valley was not much further explored until 1868 when John Wesley Powell wintered at "Powell Park," west of future Meeker. Powell's visit was a winter camp and he made few notations about the region. He was too busy preparing for his first descent down the Green River the following spring.[27]

At this same time, the question of what to do with the Utes was partly settled, for an Indian agency was set up east of Meeker to serve the region's Utes. One of the primary problems that faced settlers in northwest Colorado was the continuing occupation of the Ute Indians. By treaty, they were assured that they could live along the Yampa and White Rivers. In order to provide a homeland for the Utes, this new agency was established along the White River in 1868.[28] The White River Agency was intended to "settle" the Utes by providing education, food rations, and a subsistence based economy.[29]

While the Utes were being "taught" to farm, they continued to hunt the hills around the White River valley. This drove the agent at White River mad because the Indians were never around to do the heavy labor expected of them. When they were not hunting, they were racing horses along the banks of the White. The Utes were not interested in agriculture or a sedentary life. They much preferred to hunt and race horses, not dig ditches. Resident Indian agent, the Reverend H.E. Danforth, was much troubled by this attitude. He resigned his office in 1878, partly in disgust with the Utes, but mostly over the fact that the federal government had failed to deliver goods required by the treaty of 1873.[30]

Danforth's replacement was Nathan C. Meeker who promptly undertook the reorganization of the White River Agency. The agency was moved down river to Powell Park. Meeker decided to turn the Utes into sedentary Indians by making them farm Powell Park. To do so, he ordered that irrigation canals be built from the White River so as to water the bottomlands. The Utes were expected to do the labor and then plant crops. Meeker also established a school and a store for the Utes.

Meeker was quite displeased with the Utes' hunting habits and their desire to trade for guns at Hayden and Windsor along the Yampa River. To keep the Utes on the reservation, Meeker used their food rations as bait. While this worked, the Utes did not want to farm. Instead, they hung around the agency and raced horses. During the summer of 1879 Meeker decided that the land occupied by the Ute horsetrack had to be turned into pasture.[31] The Utes were outraged to think that their racetrack was about to be plowed under. This was during the summer of 1879 and the racing season was in full swing. Meeker offered to move the track to near the river to which the Utes replied ". . . that he could plow in another place which was further away covered by sage and greasewood, intersected by slues and badly developing alkali."[32] This referred to Meeker moving the Utes "corral" (horsetrack) away from the river and to the hills adjoining the White. This is one of the few contemporary environmental notations about the White River Agency and clearly means the upland areas that are located half a mile or more away from the river. This topography is consistent with current environmental conditions away from the river bottom. Today's vegetation is almost identical to the Utes descriptions of 1878. Sage and greasewood with gullies intersecting the land is the current condition of this region. [33]

Meeker's demands on the Utes proved to be too much. On September 30, 1879, the Indians rose in rebellion, killing Meeker and several of his male employees, taking captive Mrs. Meeker and several womean, and wiping out a detachment of U.S. Army soldiers from Fort Fred Steele, Wyoming at Milk River on the day before. The so-called Thornburgh Massacre was the end of the White River Agency. After the insurrection was quelled by federal troops, the agency was turned into an cantonment [the Cantonment on the White] that was occupied by the U.S. Army. The Utes were removed to the new Uintah reservation in Utah during 1880. Upon resettlement of the Utes, the White River Valley was opened, for the first time, to homesteaders.[34] One reason that the White River area was "ripe" for settlement was due to the explorations of Ferdinand V. Hayden.

Hayden, who in the late 1860s surveyed Yellowstone Park and was largely responsible for bring its natural wonders to the public's attention, was commissioned by the U.S. Geological Survey (USGS) to survey northwestern Colorado beginning in 1871 with Middle Park and ending with the far northwest corner by 1875 and 1876. The Hayden surveys included the Yampa and White River drainages. Sections of the reports were prepared for geology by F.M. Endlich, topography by George Chittenden and had subjects of interest such as botany, paleontology, and mineral resources.[35]

Hayden's party noted that Douglas and Piceance Creeks had constant flows, but that subsidiary creeks could not be relied upon, which made agriculture in the area risky. The expedition stated that the White River itself might have agriculture potential based on the fact that: "Mr. Danforth has cultivated about forty acres of land for use of the [White River] agency. . . .".[36] Of course, this refers to Danforth's Ute subsistence program at White River. The Hayden survey sampled about 800 square miles of land in the region and mapped the major geographic features or landmarks via the method of triangulation. Generally, they also concluded that the area was not well suited to agriculture and that without irrigation farming was not practical. They concluded that along the river bottoms grazing was possible and the land was only useful there.[37] Hayden finally concluded that the region was: ". . . nearly all uninhabitable both winter and summer. . . ."[38] Hayden notwithstanding, settlers were poised to arrive as soon as the "Ute problem" was resolved.

8

With the removal of the Utes by 1881, settlers began to fill the White River Valley. While the area was well-known to Colorado residents, thanks to previous descriptions by such explorers as Berthoud and Hayden, the land was not available until its original inhabitants were gone.

The first permanent settlement in this region was platted in 1885 when the town of Meeker was mapped and sites were sold for $2.63 each, representing the cost of filing on the land. Some of the military buildings constructed for the Cantonment on the White were sold to settlers and became the core of Meeker.[39] On the other hand, Rangely, the only other major "town" on the White was created around 1882 when C.P. Hill established a trading post along the White at Rangley.[40] By 1884 Rangely had a school and represented the westernmost village in this region. At the mouth of Piceance Creek and the White River, another town was established about 1885 called White River City. Apparently this town was founded with the hope that a proposed railroad along the White River [Berthoud's route] would be built and White River City could become a major station between Meeker and Rangely. Of course, this never happened and White River City was apparently abandoned by 1915 as indicated by the cadastral survey plats of that time.[41]

Prior to the establishment of towns during the 1880s, there were no permanent settlements in the White River region. The nearest places for mail and supplies were Rawlins, Wyoming; Windsor, Colorado; Steamboat Springs, Colorado, and Hot Sulphur Springs in Middle Park. Brown's Park in the far northwestern corner of the state was occupied by cattlemen by the mid-1860s. From that time on, some cattle grazing occurred along the White on an occasional basis.[42] The basic narrowness of the valley prevented large-scale grazing, but cattle were run up the side gulches where there was forage along the watercourses. Douglas Creek, for example, supported both cattle and sheep grazing. In fact, a cattle trail ran southerly over Douglas Pass by the mid-1880s. A route also ran along the southeast edge of the Piceance Basin from Meeker to Rifle which was the railhead by 1892. What is significant, however, is that cattle grazing in the White River valley was quite confined because of lack of forage.[43]

Much more grazing took place on the highlands around the region. Piceance Basin, Douglas Creek, Texas Creek, Philadelphia Creek, Missouri Creek, and the Yampa divide all saw cattle and later sheep grazing. James Rector, who arrived in the Douglas Creek area during the mid-1880s, described the land as: ". . . the best cow country he had ever seen—a land of lush grass, no brush, and no deep gullies or washes as are found today as a result of erosion. Douglas Creek ran on top of the ground, and you could dip water up in a bucket from in front of the cabin. White sage and blue stem grass grew 'stirrup deep' everywhere".[44]

When the first settlers arrived in the White River country, they soon discovered that the best use of the bottomlands was for irrigated agriculture. Nathan Meeker had shown this in 1879 when he watered some of the river uplands via ditches.

The General Land Office (GLO) rectangular survey plats for 1886 and 1906 show an extensive canal system west of Meeker and in Powell Park. In addition, numerous residences are shown in these plats, but farther west downriver there are very few ranches or farms indicated on the plats. Around Rangely, there are several ranches showing (i.e. Rector's), particularly to the west of that town. There were laterals extending from the river into Raven Park. All along the river, surveyors noted irrigation ditches dating from 1883 forward. Some were abandoned, some were in use. Alfalfa fields are prominently noted by several surveyors indicating that the primary use of the river bottom was for irrigated agriculture.[45] The hay/alfalfa was sold to stockraisers and horsebreeders throughout the state and nation. Canals and laterals were extended from the White to the uplands as far as possible. Willows and other vegetation along the river was a problem for settlers. Nellie Warren Parks remembered that: "Katie and Tom [Warren] moved to the mouth of Miller Creek to carve out of that wilderness of willows—a ranch. He chopped all the willows on the south side first".[46] This description is from about 1890 and continues: 'I recall that one time when Dad was cleaning off the willows and then burning them "[47] Mrs. Parks then described the fire getting away from her father and burning up the gulch. She also noted that "The only equipment that Dad had to clean this great bunch of willows was a grubbing hoe and an axe".[48]

Another description, dating from 1898, was from the Coal Creek area: "The land was virgin soil, usually covered with sagebrush and many rocks".[49] This description of the tributaries of the White is common as many settlers who arrived about 1900 found that they had to dry land farm along areas that were not irrigated. Curtis Creek, Coal Creek, Wolf Creek, Strawberry Creek, and others, including the area south of Maybell, Colorado were all settled fairly late and the descriptions are of an arid area used for dry land farming.

As settlement occurred along the White River, the bottomlands were taken up first. The majority of settlers homesteaded this region rather than purchasing the land. By the turn of the century, most of the good lands were long gone. The hillsides were not claimed because they were not useful for grazing or agriculture. Hence, they remained in the public domain under the management of the General Land Office (GLO).[50]

One of the major problems encountered along the White River was siltation. The lower reaches of the river (in Colorado) tended to carry considerable amounts of silt which clogged headgates and ditches. This is true today. James Rector's 1885 descriptions of Douglas Creek bring this fact home very clearly.

The first GLO surveys along the White River valley were done in 1883 when D.C. Oakes and J.P. Maxwell surveyed townships along the White River from Meeker to the Utah border. Later, their surveys were found to be inaccurate and were suspended. Resurveys of the defective surveys were done in 1905, 1906, and 1907. Even though inaccurate in survey terms, the 1883 survey does provide some descriptive material in the notes.[51] For example, in July 1883 Maxwell noted that the White River area was: "mountainous," and that the riverbottom soil was "alluvial, second rate, good grass."[52] He also stated that the vegetation along the river was "no timber, sagebrush scattering"[53], which is consistent with earlier descriptions of a grassy bottomland and sage covered hills. That same year surveyor Milikan noted the lower White River area as having: ". . . timber: none, sagebrush, willows. . . ."[54] The date was October 25, 1883, and he noted that there were numerous irrigation ditches along the river and that: ". . . to White River crossing, N., thence down river through thick willows. . . ."[55] This type of vegetation is consistently noted along the length of the White from Meeker westward.[56]

As homesteaders "proved up," and received title to the land, they made capital investments in ditches or canals in order to water fields that were used for hay and alfalfa production. Survey notes from the 1883 and 1905-1907 surveys consistently make note of "alfalfa fields" or grain fields along the White. The plat maps show the same features. It is clear that by 1883 irrigation and alfalfa raising was common along this river. By 1900 the majority of the land on the White was patented and in private hands. Cadastral survey plats of that time show a continuous line of private patents from Meeker to the Utah line. These represent the bottomlands, with the hillsides remaining in public domain. Changes in the riverbank and the vegetation are minimal between 1883 and 1907. Native grasses along the river bottom were replaced by domestic hay or alfalfa very early. The most notable change seems to have been the depletion of cottonwoods. Early descriptions indicate that cottonwood trees were common along the White River. Dominguez and Escalante noted them, as did the fur trappers. However, by 1868 and the time of the establishment of the White River Agency, there is little mention of cottonwoods. This is probably because most of the trees were cut down to build structures (log cabins), corrals, or for firewood.[57]

Survey descriptions of the White River area are almost devoid of references to "cottonwoods". In the 1883 survey to the 1905-1907 surveys, cottonwoods are simply not indicated. Arthur Kidder's notes of June 10, 1907, described an "island" on the White in which he crossed to get over the river while running a section line. He stated that the it was: ". . . low flat island, continue through dense undergrowth and enter heavy timber."[58] He also describes the general area as having "soil, sandy and adobe, third rate" and "timber, cottonwood: undergrowth, sage brush, greasewood and willow."[59] This is the only reference to cottonwoods found during this survey and this stand probably represented a remnant of previously timbered areas of the White. Another similar reference to cottonwoods occurs in the contemporary survey notes of William H. Clark who noted that there were "dense willows, squawberry bush (a variety of sumac) and scattering [of] young cottonwood trees in the land along the White just east of the Colorado-Utah border.[60] This would indicate that there was some regeneration of trees occurring in 1901, at the time of the survey.

The lack of large trees is consistent with historic descriptions of mining camps and settlements where trees were removed for lumber, mine timbers, charcoal and other uses. Within a few years the hills around Central City, for example, were totally denuded of trees.[61] It stands to reason the same thing happened along the White, especially west of Meeker where local trees were hard to find. The other vegetation along the White River that is consistently described in the survey notes is the presence of willows. D.C. Oakes and Milikan noted the "dense undergrowth" and "willows" along the river in 1883.[62] Later surveyors made the same comments about the White. A.H. Adams described a portion of the river thus: "Timber, scrub cedar, undergrowth, sage and greasewood, brush, and willows."[63] In 1907 Arthur Kidder stated that the area contained ". . . undergrowth, sage brush, greasewood, and willow."[64] It seems that more underbrush and willow growth existed in the 1880s and early 1900s than there is at present. Presumably the willows were removed by ranchers and hay growers to help increase field size or to help maintain irrigation ditches. In any case, the willow and cottonwood population is less today than it was historically.

Other changes along the White River since 1900 have been mostly improvements to existing features. For example, the old dirt road between Meeker and Rangley that appears on survey plats from 1900 on, has been upgraded to a state highway with appropriate encroachments upon the river in places. Several reservoirs have been built in the last 20 years. They are: Rio Blanco Lake (in the 1960s) and Taylor Draw Reservoir (1985). Both of these features are manmade. Rio Blanco Lake does not directly dam the river while Taylor Draw Reservoir does. Nevertheless, habitat along the river remains the same as historically described except around those two major man-created features. The habitat around Rio Blanco Lake is more marshy, while around the Taylor Draw Reservoir, there has been so much recent disturbance by construction that the habitat is still recovering. Mainly, it is grass and some shrubs along the reservoir floodpool with sage or greasewood on the higher levels of the shoreline. It makes sense that the upper shore is sage since the hills on either side of the river were historically described as sage covered.

Locations of the White River and its tributaries

Location Map

CONCLUSIONS

Drawing conclusions about changing environmental conditions is somewhat difficult even with good documentation available. Using descriptive materials can help paint a picture of what the riparian habitat along the White River, and its tributaries, may have looked like. Obviously, some conclusions must be, by definition, highly speculative. Nevertheless, historic writings about the region help draw an image of what it must have been like. The primary question that remains unanswered is what happened to the historical environment? The problem lies in more recent times when the historical record becomes unclear. Most recent documents note current conditions and not earlier situations. Thus, there tends to be a data gap between the end of historic records and the beginning of "modern" times.

The historic survey records end about 1910, and at that time riparian areas along the White River are very clearly lined with heavy underbrush, willows, squawberry bushes and other similar vegetation. Historically, the cottonwoods were gone by the 1890s. There may have been a few surviving groves of cottonwood trees, such as the "island" (now under Rio Blanco Lake) noted by one surveyor, but by and large, the trees were cut down by the turn of the century for use as lumber or firewood. Hence, the primary habitat for the river would have been willows, squawberry and other brushy vegetation.

This is consistent with other riparian areas in the west. River bottoms are traditionally been covered by vegetation that required considerable water, providing shelter and food for shoreline creatures like beaver, otters, and other mammals. In addition, these plants controlled soil erosion during flood periods by absorbing increased water and by providing control areas for rapidly moving water. Without cover, erosion is increased. A good example of this phenomenon can be seen along East Douglas Creek. A 1907 photograph of a homestead shows a cabin along that creek at surface level, with considerable vegetation around the stream. A photo taken about 70 years later shows that same cabin hanging over the creek, having been undercut by at least 40 feet. Soil erosion can happen quickly as this demonstrates; lack of riparian vegetation contributes to loss of soil.

The White River no longer has the same amounts of vegetation that is historically described as part of the habitat. What happened to the undergrowth and other typical riparian vegetation is documented. During the late 1920s, local ranchers removed much of the riparian area along the river in order to increase hay pasturage. For instance, in 1929 Zandy Mobley's brothers were contracted by local ranchers to clear 50 acres of cottonwoods for agricultural purposes in the area of present day Rio Blanco Lake.[64] In the mid-1940s, Mr. Mobley and his brothers cleared 60 acres of vegetation on the old Studtman place. The ranch is located about 19 miles east of Rangley on the White River, and the fields were used for irrigated agriculture.[65] We know that the river bottom was used for irrigation from at least 1883 forward. The primary crop was alfalfa which requires considerable water. It may be assumed that over the years, irrigation demands lowered the water table along the river bank and help cause the undergrowth to eventually die from lack of water. Willows and similar vegetation need a great deal of water, so even a small reduction in the flow by the White could cause the riparian zone to die. Another cause for riparian depletion is that the landowners along the White cleared the willows and other underbrush in order to enlarge their hay and alfalfa fields.[66]

The actual causes for the reduction of riparian areas along the White River are probably multiple, including lowered water table, removal of undergrowth by ranchers, increased soil erosion due to lack of cover vegetation, and other manmade modifications that caused permanent changes along the White. By the 1940s, there were russian olive and tamarack trees along the river and they have outcompeted the willows.[67] This competition could explain why the willows and other riparian vegetation mostly disappeared.

It should also be noted that public domain lands usually are not found along the bottomlands of the White. The river bottom was taken up early by settlers and has been continuously farmed since the removal of the Utes in 1881. The same is not true for the hillsides or some of the smaller drainages along the White. These lands were either never homesteaded and remained in public domain or settlement attempts failed and the land reverted to the government. The Bureau of Land

Management manages these lands which are generally no more than one half mile from the White's main channel. It is interesting to note that the historic descriptions of the uplands of the White are consistently of sagebrush and greasewood. This vegetative mix shows up in almost every report whether made in 1880 or in 1980. The lands are still sage and greasewood today. There has been little or no change for these upland areas in the last two hundred years. Based on the historic record, we can conclude that the White River drainage had a rich riparian area until sometime during the 1920s when this vegetation disappeared for various reasons. At that time, streambank erosion began and the river has slowly deepened itself due to bankside collapse. The riparian habitat that once lined the White is partly gone, and there is little to hold the banks in place. We can also conclude that the upland areas along the White have not substantially changed over the last several hundred years. It remains predominantly sage and greasewood. The greatest change that has occurred is to the riparian habitat of the White and several major tributaries such as Piceance Creek and Douglas Creek.

The White River's riparian habitat zone is today slowly recovering. There are willows along the White between Meeker and White River City, and the cottonwoods, while not yet large, are regrowing in the river's bends and along its banks. This will slow the erosion rate of the White. It is possible that today's farmers have realized the value of the original riparian habitat and are allowing it to regain a foothold.

The Taylor Draw Dam, 1985, is the only dam on the White River. (Photo by F.J. Athearn)

NOTES

1. See: Garry F. Rogers, Harold E. Malde, Raymond M. Turner. *Bibliography of Repeat Photography for Evaluating Landscape Change.* Salt Lake City: University of Utah Press, 1984; Mark Klett, et al. *Second View, The Rephotographic Project.* Albuquerque: University of New Mexico Press, 1984 and Hal G. Stevens and Eugene M. Shoemaker. *In the Footsteps of John Wesley Powell.* Boulder, Colorado: Johnson, 1987. Also see: USDI, Bureau of Land Management. *Historical Comparison Photography, Missouri Breaks, Montana.* Billings, Montana: Bureau of Land Management, 1979, and Kendall L. Johnson, *Rangeland Through Time.* Laramie: Wyoming, University of Wyoming, 1987.

2. William Henry Jackson's photographic collection now resides at the Colorado Historical Society Museum in Denver, Colorado.

3. For example, see: Quentin Skinner, "Riparian Zones Then and Now." Paper presented to Wyoming Water 1986 and Streamside Zones Conference: *Wyoming's Water Doesn't Wait While We Debate.* Laramie: University of Wyoming, 1986 and Wayne Elmore, "Riparian Management: Back To Basics." Paper Presented at Natural Resources Law Center, University of Colorado School of Law, 1987 and John C. York and William A.Dick-Peddie. "Vegetation Changes in Southern New Mexico During the Past Hundred Years," In: William G. McGinnies and Bram J. Goldman (Eds.), *Arid Lands in Perspective,* Tuscon: University of Arizona Press, 1969, pp. 157-166.

4. See: Herbert E. Bolton. *Pageant in the Wilderness: The Story of the Escalante Expedition to the Interior Basin, 1776.* Salt Lake City: Utah State Historical Society, 1951, and Herbert S. Auerbach, *Father Escalante's Journal, 1776-1777; Newly Translated With Related Documents and Original Maps.* Salt Lake City: Utah State Historical Society, 1943.

5. Fray Angelico Chavez and Ted J. Warner. *The Dominguez-Escalante Journal.* Provo, Utah: Brigham Young University Press, 1976. p. 41.

6. Ibid, p.41.

7. Ibid, pp.41-42.

8. As described in: William H. Goetzmann. *Exploration and Empire.* New York: Knopf, 1966.

9. Dale L. Morgan. *Jedediah Smith and the Opening of the West.* New York: Bobbs-Merrill, 1953.

10. Ibid., p. 188.

11. Ibid., p. 188.

12. Ibid., William H. Ashley described the region, p. 188.

13. Ibid., p. 169.

14. Ibid., p. 169.

15. Ibid., p. 167.

16. As described by F.A. Wislizenus. *A Journey to the Rocky Mountains in the Year 1839.* St. Louis: n.p., 1912. See: Frederic J. Athearn. *An Isolated Empire: A History of Northwestern Colorado.* Denver: Bureau of Land Management, 1982, p.25.

17. William H. Goetzmann. *Army Exploration in the American West, 1803-1863*. New Haven: Yale University Press, 1959. pp. 100-101. Also: John Charles Fremont. *Journal*. pp. 398-399. See also: John C. Fremont. *Memoirs*. p. 430 [as related by Goetzmann, p. 119] and Donald Jackson and Mary Lee Spence (Eds.). *The Expeditions of John Charles Fremont*. Urbana: University of Illinois Press, 1970. 4 Volumes.

18. Louise C. Harrison. *Empire and the Berthoud Pass*. Denver: Big Mountain Press, 1964.

19. Ibid., p. 14.

20. *Rocky Mountain News*. Denver, Colorado. October 12, 1861.

21. Harrison, op. cit., p. 77.

22. Ibid., p. 77.

23. Ibid., pp. 77-78.

24. Ibid., p. 77.

25. *Rocky Mountain News*. Denver, Colorado. September [?], 1866.

26. Harrison, op. cit., p. 214.

27. Goetzmann, op. cit., p. 538. See also: William C. Darrah. *Powell of the Colorado*. Princeton: Princeton University Press, 1951.

28. Robert Emmitt. *The Last War Trail*. Norman: University of Oklahoma Press, 1955, and Marshall Sprague. *Tragedy at White River*. Boston: Little, Brown and Co., 1957, and Athearn, op. cit., p. 47.

29. Athearn, op. cit., p. 48.

30 Emmitt, op. cit., pp. 53-54.

31. Ibid., pp. 149-151.

32. Marshall D. Moody. "The Meeker Massacre". *Colorado Magazine*. April, 1953, p. 95.

33. USDI, Bureau of Land Management. *Piceance Basin Resource Management Plan*. Volume 1. Meeker, Colorado: Bureau of Land Management, 1984, pp. 47-51.

34. Athearn, op. cit., p. 54.

35. Ferdinand V. Hayden. *United States Geologic Survey of the Territories. Annual Report*. 1-12. Washington, D.C.: Government Printing Office, 1867-1878. 12 Volumes. (1873), p. 81. Also: Athearn, op. cit., p. 59.

36. Hayden, op. cit., Vol. for 1876, p. 353. Also: L.F. Schmeckebier. *Publications of the Hayden, King, Powell and Wheeler Surveys*. New York: DaCapo Press, 1971.

37. Hayden, Vol. for 1875.

38. Ferdinand V. Hayden. "Explorations Made in Colorado". *American Naturalist*. Vol. XI, Number 2, 1877, pp. 73-86. Also: Richard A. Bartlett. *Great Surveys of the American West*. Norman: University of Oklahoma Press, 1962. p. 187.

39. W.D. Simms. "The Founding and Founders of Meeker". *Colorado Magazine*. October 1949, pp. 271-277.

40. Mrs. C.P. Hill. "The Beginnings of Rangley". *Colorado Magazine*. May 1934, pp. 112-116.

41. USDI, Bureau of Land Management, Survey Plats. A.H. Adams, 1906. Denver: Colorado State Office, 1988.

42. J.N. Neal. "Ranching in Rio Blanco County". *Colorado Magazine*. April, 1957. pp. 108-120 and see: John and Susan Bury (Eds.). *This Is What I Remember*. Meeker, Colorado: Rio Blanco County Historical Society, 1972.

43. Colorado State Commercial Association. "The White-Bear Country: An Undeveloped Empire". Denver: n.p., 1907. A. Dudley Gardner and Verla R. Flores (eds.). *Oral-Historical Accounts of Northwestern Colorado*. Rock Springs, Wyoming: Western Wyoming College, 1986. p.53.

44. Rio Blanco Historical Society. *This Is What I Remember, Volume II*. (Meeker, Colorado: Rio Blanco Historical Society, 1978. p. 250.

45. USDI, Bureau of Land Management. Cadastral Survey Plats and Notes. In: Colorado State Office, Denver, Colorado. Hereinafter referred to as Survey Notes, (Townships 1 and 2 North, Ranges 94 West to 104 West.)

46. Rio Blanco Historical Society, op cit., p. 154.

47. Ibid, p. 154.

48. Ibid, p.154.

49. Ibid, p.76.

50. See: Roy M. Robbins. *Our Landed Heritage*. Lincoln: University of Nebraska Press, 1942, for discussion of public land disposal policy in the United States.

51. Survey Notes. Oakes and Maxwell, 1883.

52. Survey Notes. Maxwell, July 1883.

53. Survey Notes. Maxwell, July 1883.

54. Survey Notes. Milikan, 1883.

55. Survey Notes. Milikan, October 1883.

56. Survey Notes. 1883 and 1906.

57. See: Mary D. Oldland. "Sixty Seven Years in the White River Valley". *Colorado Magazine*. July, 1952. pp. 195-201.

58. Survey Notes. Arthur D. Kidder, June 1907.

59. Survey Notes. Kidder, June 1907.

60. Survey Notes. William H. Clark, May 1901.

61. For a detailed description of environmental devastation by mining see: Duane A. Smith. *Colorado Mining*. Albuquerque: University of New Mexico Press, 1977.

62. Survey Notes. D.C.Oakes and Milikan, 1883.

63. Survey Notes. Alonzo H. Adams, June 1907.

64. Survey Notes. Arthur Kidder, November 1907.

65. Interview with Zandy Mobley, March 7, 1988. Conducted by Michael Selle, Meeker, Colorado. (Mr.Mobley is lifelong Rio Blanco County resident).

66. Ibid.

67. Interview with Mrs. Charles Deveraux, March 2,1988. Interview conducted by Michael Selle, Meeker, Colorado. (Mrs. Deveraux is a lifelong Rio Blanco County resident who was raised on a ranch along the White River. She lived on the White until 1943 when her family moved.)

APPENDIX 1
PHOTOGRAPHIC PLATES

PLATE 1

Photo Number 1. E.T. Hancock #13, 1911. (U.S. Geological Survey Photo). Syncline at head of Sulphur [Curtis] Creek.

PLATE 2

Photo Number 1. F.J. Athearn, 1988. The habitat is the same as the 1911 photo except for the ranch in the center of the 1988 photo, and Highway 13 in the foreground. Sagebrush has encroached since 1911, otherwise there is little vegetative change. Hancock misidentified this drainage as Sulphur Creek.

PLATE 3

Photo Number 2. E.T. Hancock # 36, 1911. (U.S. Geological Survey Photo). Sulphur Creek Mine.

PLATE 4

Photo Number 2. F.J. Athearn, 1988. The Sulphur Creek Mine is gone, replaced by a sawmill. The drainage is no longer under cultivation and has revegetated to native and annual grasses. The brush species in the background has increased since 1911.

PLATE 5

Photo Number 3. H.S. Gale #162, no date. (U.S. Geological Survey Photo). Panorama showing the Mesa Verde ledge on north side of the White River, just below Meeker.

PLATE 6

Photo Number 3. F.J. Athearn, 1988. The trees in the foreground of the above photo have been removed. Sagebrush has encroached in the foreground, while the background trees, seen above, were cut to increase hay production. Highway 13 between Meeker and Rifle is to the right and does not show in the Gale photo.

PLATE 7

Photo Number 4. H.S. Gale # 163, no date. (U.S. Geological Survey Photo). Panorama showing the Mesa Verde ledge on the north side of the White River, just below Meeker.

PLATE 8

Photo Number 4. F.J. Athearn, 1988. The trees in the middle ground have been removed for hay field enlargement. Sagebrush is encroaching in the near foreground. This photo was taken from the south side of a new county road that showes in the immediate foreground.

PLATE 9

Photo Number 5. J.T. Eby # 197, 1924. (U.S. Geological Survey Photo). Escarpment Peak looking northwest from the divide between Strawberry Creek and the Keystone Basin.

PLATE 10

Photo Number 5. F.J. Athearn, 1988. Dryland wheatfield, at right of photo, is in the Eby photo also. The erosional pattern is much the same as in the 1924 view. Eby's photo indicates that the wheatfield has just been cleared for production.

PLATE 11

Photo Number 6. J.A. Davis # 2, 1908. (U.S. Geological Survey Photo). Piceance Creek below
the Alees Ranch, ca. 1908.

PLATE 12

Photo Number 6. F.J. Athearn, 1988. There has been a complete vegetative change from sub-irrigated grassland (possibly hay) to a dry, sagebrush annual weed type plant community.

PLATE 13

Photo Number 7. W.H. Bradley # 159, 1925. (U.S. Geological Survey Photo). View down Piceance Creek from Section 11, Township 1 North, Range 97 West. July 28,1925.

PLATE 14

Photo Number 7. F.J. Athearn, 1988. There is little change from 1925 except for sagebrush encroachment which has hidden Piceance Creek from view.

PLATE 15

Photo Number 8. H.S. Gale #324, no date. (U.S. Geological Survey Photo). Mouth of Red Wash, from the south side of the White River.

PLATE 16

Photo Number 8. F.J. Athearn, 1988. The earlier agricultural endeavor has been abandoned and the field has reverted to native brush, grass, and annual weeds.

PLATE 17

Photo Number 9. H.S. Gale #318, no date. (U.S. Geological Survey Photo). White River Valley. Taken at the mouth of Wolf Creek.

PLATE 18

Photo Number 9. F.J. Athearn, 1988. The original photo indicates that vegetation along the creek is in a very depleated condition. Sagebrush has encroached and matured to the point that the creek is no longer visable.

PLATE 19

Photo Number 10. H.S. Gale # 366, no date. (U.S. Geological Survey Photo). View across the White River Valley at the upper end of Raven Park from Section 32, Township 2 North, Range 101 West.

PLATE 20

Photo Number 10. F.J. Athearn, 1988. There is little evident change except where the trees have greatly increased at the base of the escarpment. Modern buildings and an airport are now in the foreground.

PLATE 21

Photo Number 11. H.S. Gale # 334, no date. (U.S. Geological Survey Photo). Panoramic view of the White River Valley in Raven Park. Taken from the south side of the river....

PLATE 22

Photo Number 11. F.J. Athearn, 1988. This photo shows the town of Rangley in the foreground. There are many more trees along the White River than in the Gale photo.

PLATE 23

Photo Number 12. H.S. Gale # 371, ca. 1907. The N Bar Ranch and the Monument Peak in the background. This is situated in the main forks of Douglas Creek.

PLATE 24

Photo Number 12. F.J. Athearn, 1988. The ranch in the foreground of the Gale photo is gone. They may have been growing hay in sub-irrigated pastures. East Douglas Creek has eroded greatly since 1907. The ranch that appeared in 1907 is now totally gone having been undercut by bank erosion.

PLATE 25

Photo Number 13. Bureau of Land Management/Western Wyoming College, 1974. This is the last building of the N Bar Ranch remaining as of 1974. This structure is seen the lower right corner of the 1907 Gale photo. The stream has undercut the ranch and this log cabin is about to collapse into the wash. The building is gone as of 1988.